To Lily —

I am so glad you are having so much fun at dance with me. I love you bunches and I hop you enjoy the book.

♡ always,
Auntie Mel ☺

SOMETIMES I JUST WANT TO DANCE

Written and Illustrated by Melissa Medeiros
Edited by William V. Ciaccio

Sometimes I Just Want to Dance

Published by PCG Kids
317 Appaloosa Trail
Waco, TX 76712

ISBN: 978-1-936417-43-8

Printed in the United States of America

Contact the Author: www.uniquesteps.com

This Book Belongs To: _____

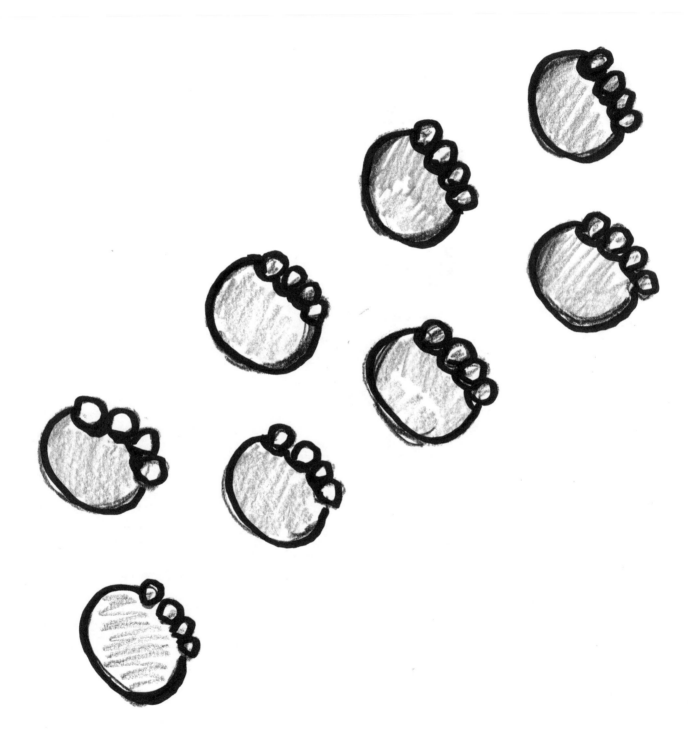

In loving memory of my grandmother,
Grace, who was such an inspiration to me.

And to Billy——without you, this book would
never have been completed.

Ellie was a sweet, silly, six-year-old elephant with lots of energy, big thoughtful brown eyes, and a lovely smile. She lived in a house with her mother, her father, and her grandmother, Grace.

Ellie loved to do lots of things. She loved to paint the flowers in her mother's garden, she loved to sing her favorite songs. She also loved playing with her friends, but most of all she loved to dance.

Ellie danced everywhere. She danced when she woke up in the morning. She danced in the kitchen. She danced while she brushed her teeth; she even danced in the grocery store aisles!

Ellie found it hard to concentrate in school. She could not control the tapping of her feet. Ellie's feet would click and tap on the floor.

Her teacher would turn from the blackboard with a stern, disapproving look and say, "Please stop tapping your feet, Ellie."

Ellie would waltz home
from school while her
mother was making dinner
and twirl into the kitchen.

Ellie came waltzing into the room telling her mother about her day. Her mother, being too focused on a simmering bamboo stew and a peanut desert would say, "Ellie, what are you doing?"

Ellie replied, "Sometimes, Momma, I just want to dance!"

"Well, please don't do it right now, I am trying to cook."

One bright sunny day while Ellie was dancing in the yard, her grandmother came out and said, "Stop trampling the flowers and help me in the market!"

When they arrived at the grocery store, Grandma was looking in the produce section when she realized Ellie was no longer standing next to her. She turned around to see her tip toeing around the zucchinis.

"Ellie?" her grandmother asked, "What are you doing?"

"Sometimes, Grandma," Ellie replied, "I just want to dance!"

"Well, you cannot do it in the store!" she said disapprovingly.

When they returned home, father was relaxing in front of the television, watching the nightly news. Ellie came leaping into the room and frolicked in front of the TV set.

Father exclaimed, "Ellie, what are you doing?"

"Sometimes, Papa, I just want to dance!" Ellie replied.

"Well, you cannot do it in the living room while I'm trying to watch television," he said.

Ellie was sad.

If she could not dance
in the living room while
father was watching
television, she was not
supposed to dance in the
kitchen while mother
was cooking, she was
certainly not allowed
to dance at the grocery
store, and she could not
dance at school...what
would she do?

She just wanted to
dance.

Just as she sat in her room wondering what to do, there was a knock at the door. It was Grace, her grandmother. "Ellie," Grandma said, "I've got a really special surprise for you. I know how much you love to dance so I bought you a present."

Ellie opened the box to find a beautiful little pair of pink ballet slippers and a brand new leotard.

Ellie was so excited and the Grandma said, "I know how much you love to dance so I've bought you ballet shoes and an outfit and tomorrow you start dance class."

Ellie jumped in the air. She could most certainly dance at dance class. Ellie ran downstairs to tell her mother and father who already knew about the surprise.

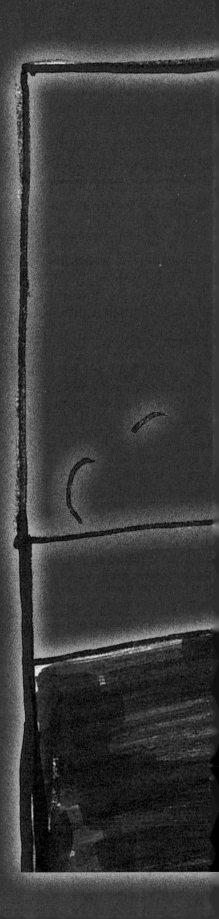

"See," Momma said, "We love that you want to dance, we just needed to find you a place to do it." And Ellie smiled.

All she wanted to do was dance.

Some of Ellie's Favorite Ballets that I've Seen:

- ☐ Coppelia
- ☐ Sleeping Beauty
- ☐ Swan Lake
- ☐ The Nutcracker
- ☐ Giselle
- ☐ La Bayadere

Pictures of Other Ballerinas

My Dance Pictures

Don't you just want to dance?

Melissa Medeiros was born and raised in
Massachusetts. Melissa has made a career and a
life thanks to the art of dance. She currently has
a BFA in Dance from Dean College and a Master's
in Expressive Therapies from Lesley University
in Cambridge, Ma. She currently owns Unique
Steps Dance Academy located in North Attleboro,
Massachusetts and also works as a clinician
working towards her LMHC.